MW01105274

NATIVE SONG

POETRY AND PAINTINGS

by

DAVID WOODS

Pottersfield Press

Lawrencetown Beach, Nova Scotia

Pottersfield Press
RR #2 Porters Lake
Nova Scotia, Canada
B0J 2S0

Woods, David A. 1959 —
  Native Song

  Poems
  ISBN 0-919001-61-0

I. Title.

PS8595.062N37 1990 C811'.54 C90-097628-4
PR9199.3.W66N37 1990

Some poems of this collection have appeared previously in *Poetry Halifax Dartmouth, Community, The Preserver, Black Express, The Jet, The Daily News*, and *The North-end News*.

Cover Painting: "Cain" by David Woods
Photographs of the paintings by George Georgakakos

This book was produced with the financial assistance of Multiculturalism Canada - The Secretary of State for Multiculturalism and Citizenship.

Special thanks to Sylvia Hamilton, Richard Raymond and Fred Ward for their support and encouragement.

Many of the people, names, and situations represented in this work are fictional creations of the author.

Pottersfield Press receives block grant funding from The Canada Council and the Nova Scotia Department of Tourism and Culture

TABLE OF CONTENTS

Discovery

Beauty's Eye
(For Annette)

I am inside someone
who is beautiful.
I look out of his eyes
Feel the vast areas of
his strength
See the horizons of his
possibilities.

A human thing — once maimed
Beaten into out-cast dungeons,
Where the self was made to feel
less than human,
Where ugliness was twisted into
the soul,
Till like a tree — I uncovered
my own roots
And shook powerfully in the sun.

(It was a beautiful feeling
Glowing through the midnight forest,
It moved like a magician
Into the dark chambers of my heart.)

It is a human love I dream inside,
A beautiful palace you trivialize
As mere words or irrelevant feeling.
But it contains all of my meaning.

And as the Sun —
Moves into the dark forest
where I have remained,
Discovers me — a sleeping child
Cold, trembling, waiting.
Understands my pain and
stretches forth its rays.

As the Sun is Love
It nourishes the thing inside me,
And I sprout forth with so much
beauty —
The Sun screams!

EVANGELINE

(For Preston)

I will not forbid this love,
How it wanders like a gentle stream
into private corners,
Or caresses lonely wounds
Like a mother's hands,
Till a vision is picked up
And fed to my hungry soul.

It may be delusion
To dream so wantonly,
Or to be so captured by
Sweetened scents of beauty,
As to enter this troubling realm,
Though the soul suckles continually
to such wants.

Yet unquieted by night,
A burning thought rouses the soul
from sleep,
Pushes the limbs out of hesitation,
Till at last brave —
I pick up books, bags and coat
And go with naked energy —
To the source of my inspiration.

PRESTON

Our beauty lies in it,
Though it often fronts a face of horror
That darkens my eyes with shame.

Our hopes and dreams enrich
its every corner,
Though it often fails to bloom
And leaves me tangled in a mass of despair.

Our wills to God illuminate its
every track,
Though it often loses the light
And I am again devoured by darkness.

Yet this is the measure of all
for which we stand,
A native-land —
Wealthy with beauty, comedy,
joy, romance,
Moves with its own style
against the dint of the modern world.

And in Sunday ritual —
Vibrant faces lift their voices
into sacred song,
A beautiful celebration of spirit —
that pierces the metal of the world,
And loosens its iron heart to love.

TO ROSELLA

In time —
When the mind settles
into its fleshy abode,
When the feet tire
And the eyes slowly close,
There will be a star
Lighting the vast darkness
of night,
And that star will be you.

I know a girl —
I know a girl,
She is a world,
A beautiful being,
In a harsh setting,
And if I could set
this life to task,
Then it would be to erect tall monuments
that would celebrate:
Each strand of her beautiful hair
 — Each movement of her slender body,
 — Each mood that seizes her magical eyes,
And I would work tirelessly —
Through summer's heat
And winter's rage —
To capture each fragment of her beauty,
So that the world may have it all.

For Rosella
I love you dearly,
And if it is God
Who decides love in this world,
Then I thank Him so much
For making me blessed.

For in a world
Of cold, terrible things,
Where a man often stands battered,
Alone, empty within,
There are those things which
lift the head upwards —

Cause the heart to pulse,
Give new life to tired limbs.

And when I have risen
from sadness,
To again set my hands to tasks,
And when in their pursuit,
I find love and happiness
light a path in the dark,
Then I know —
I exist in this world
Because in it there is someone
like you.

LUMINERE

Praise men and women
who were slaves,
Praise their toil and their love-making,
Praise their defiance and their shameful
servitude,
Praise when they bled from whip- wounds,
And when in courage
they lifted their feet into flight.

Praise when they mothered children,
Praise when they brought their babies
to strength with love,
Praise when they scoured puzzling books
in search of wisdom,
And when their voices
raised joy-filled melodies into the night.

Praise their comraderie and their simple
pride,
Praise their ecstatic dances and their
fanciful flights,
Praise when they transformed cruelty to
love —
And darkness to light,
And praise when they called to God in
the sky
And He came down in a burst of glory
To open a path to freedom before their eyes.

FOR SLAVES

Slaves are my Gods,
Titans of pained worlds,
Builders of new earth,
How they braved in unloved ambition,
And toiled in loveless sun,
How they fuelled the glory of
other men's dreams,
And constructed palaces of wonder,
For those less than themselves.

How they felled trees and
lifted stone,
How they nursed children
and tended herds,
How they stayed late in
midnight rooms —
And lifted their eyes towards heaven:
Dreaming of a pure and gentle earth —
Where all lived in freedom.

BIDII (The Flight)

About blackness
I never had doubt,
My need to enter the lives
of slaves
And give expression to their
every voice.
(A black bird surmounts the sky,
It sees its murdered beauty —
And issues a loud, despondent cry).

Call this romantic mulct
for a deluded head,
Or irrelevant fetish,
Or claim — the lost soul
confused in its motives —
Closes into a useless empire
in order to hide.

(Yet how would you know —
when you were the vulture
tearing at my flesh —
With steel claws and fiery eyes,
Raping me of innocence
And leaving my paths strewn with lies?)

I prefer to say —
A black soul — bloated by torture,
Folds as a sickly child
Under the weight of its oppressor's eyes.
Lost then, without nerve,
It wallows in self-hatred,
Till memory serves and reveals
the glory that once lay in life.

As the memory is sun —
It opens the man inside of me
Basks my mind in new energy.
Till cocky and confident —
I cast aside human chains,
Lift up my imagination —
And like a pair of wings —
Takes to the skies.

HEROES

A soul —
Bigger than man —
More precious than gold,
Collects with a secret prescription,
The proudest elements of the world.

No one can comprehend —
When it is found,
It appears suddenly,
In a flash of beauty,
That is the centre of truth —
The fabric of heaven.

EXTRAORDINAIRE

(For Rev. Richard Preston)

This man climbed great mountains
when it was unheard of,
Lifted weights from downed heads,
Travelled far and wide
with a light-giving eye,
Gave hope to the abandoned
in their dark chambers,
Opened the gates of possibilities,
Freed the imagination inside
stunted minds,
Shaped the face of mirth and intelligence,
A founder of institutions
A doer of deeds
A human!

ASSERTIVE

Build from small things
great nations,
Not for usury,
Not for hate,
Not for edification of
false value.
Build from flesh, and stone
and rubble —
Houses of passion that create.
Let their waves inspire the young
And their creations
Bring the old to new flame.
Pull from the locked chambers
The unsilenced yearnings,
And from the diligent
The energetic flame.
Sew new thread into the
muscles of the soul
Deliberate!

REALITY SONGS

ELSIE DORRINGTON

Elsie Dorrington —
Never had it on her mind,
She was just another girl
in the twelfth grade
With a cute smile and
sprouting breasts.

But she got tired of the way
people kept looking at her,
Tired of the stupid things friends could
and did say,
Tired of "Nigger" on the walls
And insults in the halls.

And so she did this terrible, terrible thing,
— to keep her soft mind
— to protect her young heart
— to keep the tears from her eyes,
Started this street-walking, hand-slapping,
loud-talking thing,
Put on these tight, tight pants —
And became exactly as they said.

Now everybody's talking about
how bad Elsie Dorrington is.
"But she used to be so nice,"
I hear them say.
But I wonder if they ever
got tired
(Of being nobody when you really are somebody)
I mean real tired?

FOR BERNICE JOHNSON

Face in cold grey —
Window-head watching
The movement of arms, feet,
day —
Across her weary-will,
Staring fat, alone
and still.

What can I say —
As I flit casually by?
What can I say
Dressed in elegant suit and tie?
"Good morning Mrs. Johnson,"
A less formal "Hi,"
Or moved by sudden passion
cry:
"The ignorant soul may not
know or see a prison,
But is nevertheless bound by,
Mrs. Johnson, I can see that you
live in a prison
And your life has been a lie!"

And continue:
"That man whom you call your husband,
That man who rapes and beats you at will,
That man with too little food for his vain
ego,
Is your lie."

And even more cruel add:
"For Bernice I see that you have given
Given up your arms, and teeth and hair,
Given up your vagina and soft breasts,
Given up your proud face, and pleasant ways,
To this male want
To his many children
To his lies.
I wonder if you have seen him
Fat and monied,
Walking through the streets
With young whores at his side?"

"Oh Bernice
To think of your life
Once lit up by dreams,
To think of your face
Once radiant with pride,
I remember you in beauty
I remember you in sure stride.
Do you ever think
Or are you so satisfied,
To sit, to linger, to stare, to die
To become an ugly monument
to poverty and sadness
Tossed before the world's uncaring eyes?"

I consider saying all this —
As I flit casually by,
When under a heavy breath —
I hear my useless voice whisper:
"Hi."

FOR STARR JONES
(Woman In Sorrow)

I have heard her cry
from the tear-stained room,
I have seen her devotion
to an aroused male fool,
I have seen her naked
Sit silent on a bed,
I have seen her in desperation
Fall to her knees in prayer.

(I have seen her often —
And listened to her cry.)

And I have seen her
In thin clothes dress and go,
I have seen a waiting winter
toss her to and fro,
I have seen her dishevelled
brought before an uncaring eye,
I have seen her beaten back
to her room to cry.

(I have seen her often —
And listened to her cry)

And it brings me to mad blood —
Brings me to the cruel eye,
That goes angrily to the tragic room
in which she hides,
Opens its door, roams about
its tables,
Drinks its cheap wine,
Listens to her excited talk of love and God,
In which her battered mind hides.
Delusions! Lies!
While the burden of poverty wears her thin,
While the sting of loneliness
Hits like a whip against her skin.

There are no dreams here for Starr,
No easy schemes into which she can toss
her frail body,

There is no God —
No love
No hope.
Dreamfilled Starr in a room
is a lie,
A mere object locked in a wheel
that decides
All there is to decide,
A wheel made of hard cruel steel,
A wheel whose hunger is for flesh
And whose contentment is in death,
A wheel that turns in a relentless
will —
To which she comes delivered
In her thin clothes
In her half-baked schemes.
To which she comes delivered
In her escapist religion
In her groundless hopes and dreams.
To which she comes delivered
Spread prostrate on a bed.

I have heard her often
And listened to her cry,
And all this I have seen
in those narrow, tear-filled eyes.

HARVEY BARTON AT THE TAVERN

Harvey Barton goes to the tavern,
Sixty-five years old but still
held by its pulse,
Tap shoes on his feet
Long, ridiculous scarf,
Alcoholic regret in his veins,
He is excited — it shows on
his face,
This place still gives him the spark
for living.

He has come here countless
times before,
First as a young man from
the country —
Handsome to a fault,
Now bald, arthritic
He no longer cares for display,
He has his passion for dancing
Most else has faded away.

The stage is set
His name is called,
And there is an old girlfriend Trudy
And there is a cousin — Rob,
Tap! Tap ! The feet begin
The untalented beating upon
Life's huge drum.

He is a little ridiculous
But that does not matter,
His dance is understood
by all those gathered,
From the sturdy labourers
of Hammonds Plains,
To the young hookers
from "the Square,"
His feet tell their tales
Of simple lives gone wrong,
Of wasted beauty and ruined
families

Of the simple and the poor —
Locked in an uncaring community.

He stays too long
And there is a bit of a fuss,
From someone who is perhaps too bitter,
Someone who is perhaps a little drunk,
But he is given applause
And flattered by kisses,
And what else — I ask
can we offer
To someone reaching his journey's end?
But to give him the stage —
Amid a gathering of friends.
Shower him with applause —
Before the performance ends.

MAMA
(For Delilah Reddick)

After all what mama said
Should have been expected,
Grandma dying an alcoholic
death,
Cousin Tony in jail,
Aunt Margaret on the verge of
going insane,
These things had been laid out
in some pre-ordained scheme,
Waiting for those who no longer
press the fuse, or reach
beyond the narrow boundaries
of Guysborough County.

And here I am
Talking to my mama,
Who has come 200 miles
through snow and pelting rain,
To sit for a while, admire my house
gossip, complain,
Till in the midst of her energetic
outpourings,
She pauses a while and reveals
a look of intense pain.

Guysborough County —
How my mind hollered out
of its black woods,
desperate loneliness,
and cold shacks,
How my dreams wanted out of its
family entanglements, blunted love
and white aggression.
To enter more truly the world
With an idea of being free,
I have arrived at this point
Yet something remains crying
and unfinished in me.

Someone should care for black
people

Someone should speak for their
long-cherished hopes and dreams,
Someone should rebel against
their hideous oppression in white towns.
Here is my mother —
And she intimates me to this pain.

"And you remember Mrs. Desmond's girl
Daisy,
Well she's living with this old man
in Tracadie."

"And Anna Morris is getting married
in New Glasgow,
Her husband's a drunkard, though."

"And Cousin Viola got some kind
of blood disease,
The church is having a fund-raiser
to send her for an operation in Toronto."

And what more can I say to her?
What more can I do?
But to sit and listen enthusiastically,
Shake my head, offer another cup
of coffee,
Knowing her horror full-well:
She is afraid and does
not want to go back.
Yet I cannot offer her
What she must have
To free her unease:
A chance to redo her life —
A chance like me
to escape completely.

And after a while
Tired of my impregnable
manner,
She packs her things
and leaves,
Assured in herself of having
fulfilled some sacred task,
I imagine her

as she arrives back:
"I was up to see my David
He's quite handsome
and doing fine,
Him and the wife will be
up at Christmas
Angie, he asked for you
to write."

The train taking her back
Whips through the long blackness
of Colchester and Pictou Counties,
Through scenes made macabre —
By the onslaught of a winter storm,
She is there
Huddled in a coat —
Sleeping — like a child
Till a sudden stop throws her out
At the Guysborough Station,
And she stands here
Alone and aghast,
There is no one to meet her,
And she argues with Bill and Uncle Harold
on the phone,
Till her voice breaks into
a shrill cry,
And she crumples into a pile
As a final Blackness comes
down on her eyes,
Mama,
Mama.

BRIDGETOWN

No one came to Mrs. Johnson's funeral,
Save a gaunt, white man
Who had been her employer,
Her children scattered and
unforgiving,
Her store without wares,
The sun hushed into another
"Valley" evening,
And all was soon forgotten.

Mr. Warrington
Pestered by an intelligent
mind,
Tried to save the old church
Long deserted by reverend and
congregation alike.
He argued fiercely with town
officials,
Yet could not coy out of
the gone wood
It's once resonant glory,
Nor convince minds bent
on modernity,
Out of their intended destruction.

Four hooligans from Middleton,
Burned the Old Mill to a
useless pile,
Young and outside connection
They could not see the vast
stores of memories
Held in those walls,
Nor care for the fire —
They had extinguished in old men's
eyes.

A young man — foreign born,
Spoke at the Hall
When there were only thirty
people left "on the Road,"
He spoke of community development —
He spoke of cultural revival —

He spoke of the sins endured by people
in days of old,
The old men — enlivened
by the occasion,
Clapped fervently —
Then headed for the tavern
across town,
Where laughter and old bards
poured forth —
Intimating one with feelings
incredibly sacred and
proud.

Mr. Warrington —
Sitting apart as usual,
Belaboured over a point
brought up in light conversation
Drowning our soul in
darkness,
Till a well-delivered anecdote
Yanked a smile from his agonized face,
The music upkept the revelry —
Yet could not banish a thought
growing in his mind:
That behind all this expression of rural
beauty,
Lay a vast, horrible lie.

NOVA SCOTIA REALITY SONG

In North Preston today
Ingram Byard married Marion Downey,
Ingram is called "Butch," Marion — "Mainey,"
(After the tradition of nicknaming that
exists in that community),
The reception was held in Dartmouth,
With the women resplendent in white and green

But some white men passing
Flicked ugliness into the scene:
"Look at them niggers!" they shouted,
And made my soul scream.

I CRY —
Feeling the depth of black pain.

In 1852,
An African Baptist Church was organized in
Halifax,
The African Baptist Church is a church for
black people,
A black church was needed because
the white church closed its doors,
"Negroes smell and sing too loud,"
Whites complained,
And set off a petition to the Bishop and the
King.

I CRY —
Feeling the depth of black pain.

In 1947
Viola Desmond was arrested
At the Graceland Theatre in New Glasgow,
Viola had gone that evening to see her
favourite show,
In New Glasgow a law forbid blacks from
sitting in the downstairs section,
It was reserved for whites only.
They wanted her to go upstairs
Because it was the balcony —
They called it "A Nigger's Heaven."

37

I CRY —
Feeling the depth of black pain

In 1962 —
The city of Halifax approved the destruction
of Africville,
Africville was a black community on the rim
of the Bedford Basin,
It was founded in the 1800s and ignored by
the city.
There was no sewage,
   — no lights,
   — no sidewalks
   — no water
In Africville,
The people did the best they could —
Building from their dreams and industry
They built a church — houses for their families.
Starting in 1960 they listened as their homes
were called "shacks,"
Their community, "Canada's worst slum,"
By 1969 houses, church, people were all gone.

I CRY —
Feeling the depth of black pain.

Mary Desmond
Looked out of the squalor of her country
room,
Room that was cold, dark and lonely,
Heard the shouts of her crying child.
Felt the sharp movements inside her swollen
belly,
Reached out from the pain
She suddenly grabbed for some area of peace,
Pounded against the swell
And killed the substance of her unborn child
I heard her cry out from pain.

And I CRY —
Feeling the depth of black pain.

Where is my way in Nova Scotia?

In whose words will I find my comfort?
In whose love-filled hands will I find my peace?
I cry out for dignity.
Must it always be to go and so
continually hear
Words of insult tossed cruelly
into the air?
Must it always be to go and so
continually see
The destruction of things
dear to me?
I beat inside a black skin
Stare out from inside a black brain,
I was there at the moment of
Butch's marriage to Mainey,
I was there when the white church closed its
doors,
I was there when Viola Desmond was arrested,
I was there when Africville was taken,
I was there when Mary Desmond killed her
child,
I was there at those moments,
And I am there now,
Feeling their weight press against me —
Feeling their substance pulse through my
veins.

I attempt to defeat them —
I attempt to keep them in place,
But with each new turn
That brings another cruel voice
Or hate-filled face,
I feel these scenes awake
again and again,

And I am forced to cry —
Feeling the depth of black pain.

SYMPATHY'S PEOPLE

Old Mrs. Grange
Fed her well-suffered soul
to community service,
Organized church picnics
and church fairs and
unheeded reunions,
Received an award from
Our illustrious mayor,
Gave speeches at the local
sorority clubs,
And generally oppressed everyone.

(Sympathy's People
Who never own, create or
control
But merely respond to someone
else's impulses,
Twist in someone else's shadows.)

And Reggie Cromwell —
Gifted with intelligence and
elegant looks,
Caused proud discussion
among young and old alike
Who, impressed by his rising success,
Elevated his achievements to grandiose heights.
But falling to drink —
He soon deserted intelligent energies,
And became content to take a job
at the local mill,
And press the last splinters
of his wisdom
Into heated conversations on useless topics
Around the tables at the bar.

(Sympathy's People)

And the people of Hassett
Old and backward in their ways,
Summoned long-darkened energies
and constructed a wonderful new church,
Which caused the emotional Rev. Bright

to proclaim,
"This is a new beginning for
coloured people."
Though the young remained outside
Stern and unimpressed,
Staring from long faces that seemed
shadowed by death.

(Sympathy's People)

And so — as always —
Summer silenced into winter,
And white winter dropped on us again,
With the usual turning of leaves
And other incidents that go with
those changes:
Rev. Bright was always good
for a sermon,
Old Mrs. Grange — for a speech,
There would always be dances at
the Legion,
Liquor and cheap women at Keith's.

(Sympathy's People)

And when the Miller band
Played the tired strings
of a country song
At another Legion dance.
Laughter and old bards
peeled into the midnight air,
As the old folks danced
And drowned themselves in beer.

The young boys waited for them in cars,
A look of anger invading their eyes,
As they glimpse in this scene
their special curse:
That soon all the rage-passion
of their youth —
Would expire into this drunken dross.

(Sympathy's People)

THE VILLAGE FOOL

He got "sweeet-man"
painted on his car,
He got seven children
by seven different women so far,
He got women lined up from
uptown to downtown,
He can purr like Billy Dee
And howl like James Brown.

He got the latest American tapes
And talks in the latest American slang,
He got imported suits from New York
And his cologne can leave you in a trance.

He rises early
Seven days a week,
from sun-up to sun-down
He's polishing his shoes —
Making sure his tires don't squeak.
He spends a lot of time
Maintaining his cool,
Cause it takes a lot of energy
to be a village fool.

THE DESPERATE TURN TO DANCE

Amy loves to dance
Fling herself into wild romance,
She goes with a man named
Dan,
He drives a fancy car
And smokes a big cigar,
Party, party
Till morning light.
Children at home —
Waiting for love,
"Derby," "Picadilly,"
"After-hours Club,"
And this is what she calls
life,
And this is what he calls
life.

We turn in a sad, sad
core,
The more we dance
The more desperate it becomes,
But there is beauty
in desperation:
Freak-dance, wild romance,
Fancy-curls, excited girls.
Beauty in desperation
But a horror in death to which
it leads.

CITY (1980)

Breaking in the city —
Where we confront the
solid structures of reality,
Structures no hipness can beat —
Structures no quick dream easily defeats.
From the cold air, a harsh voice descends:
"And where will you live boy?"
"On Gottingen Street, sir
Where poverty reigns."
"And where will you work boy, speak loudly
so I can hear!"
"For Modern Building Cleaners, sir —
Cleaning foul stairs."
"And where will you go when the weekend
comes?"
"I shall go to the lowly Hunter's Tavern, sir —
To dance with friends."

FOR "PIXIE" BEALS

After a while —
Tired of dragging herself
through low-paying jobs
and dusty streets,
Tired of dead-end lovers
and burnt-out dreams,
Pixie picks up and
moves to Montreal —
In angered admission —
"Place can't do nothing
for me,
Got to go, get out of
here,
Men are bums."

Got to watch it though —
Actors often re-arrange
the scene
When the piece isn't working,
Bigger cast, more elaborate setting,
Still, the girl who wanders blindly onto the
stage,
With no rehearsed lines, no obvious talent
Remains consistent
The lost is the lost!

CREIGHTON AVENUE DREAMS
(For Barry Lucas)

Those fierce days
driving about in cars,
Moving through the frenetic jungle
of Project streets
With a steeled anger and muscled
nerve.
Pressing for effect in the locomotive
ease of the world,
Deferring all serious concern for
the thrill of now.

One must understand
The mouth from which we come,
What pain-savaged ground
spawned us,
Young, held in foul corners.
Ruined early — attended by young lovers,
Offering a sensual, unruly prize,
Pushed into bold response
Nourished by sensual, unruly lies.

We went on that summer —
In a blaze that made us fly,
While the wild streets of our alienation —
Waited like knives for our nascent flesh,
The pretend power we had in our
machines
Kept us tough — and took us to
a high plateau of dreams.
Till a sudden drop of earth
Belied the notion —
And rolled us to our deaths.

MELDA'S BLUES

She romanticized her yearnings —
Yet the freedom she found
in dance
Could not be repeated in the
grimy corners of reality.

Her romance, for example,
Could not stop her father from leaving,
The white man from refusing to rent,
Or her sister Lucie from becoming
a whore.

VOICES

Exclamation

Oh Lord! Oh Lord!
My little Mary had a baby!
Oh Lord! Oh Lord!
She went an done it —
Fore she turn a lady!

Love

"I love that girl so much
My hair getting kinkier"

Report

Mary and Darren
Was both so ugly,
The reverend refused to
marry them,
On the grounds that
it wouldn't be fair
to their children.

The Reverend

They accused the Reverend
of drinking up the Church
cheap wine,
Then they accused him of
messin' with the congregation
women,
When they finally accused him
of stealing from the Church
Building Fund,
The Reverend got mad and
burned the Church down!

My Father

My father read the Bible
Each night before he
went to bed,
Then he would down a
shot of whisky
That kicked like a donkey
through his head.
And to this day
No word of a lie,
No one's sure if it's the religion
or the whisky,
Keeping that old man alive.

Rufus Peters

Rufus Peters
got Mrs. Saunder's 15 year old
pregnant,
Despite being married
and a respected deacon
in the church.
Well "Ole Ruf" denied,
denied and denied
But nine months later
Them spacey teeth
On Missie's child,
Sure proved that deacon
had lied.

Incident

At the Ebony Club last night
John Sparks and Henry Grosse
Got into a terrible fight,
They beat on each other's heads,
And would not cease,
And so the manager picked up the phone
And called the police,
But when the men in blue came,

And much to everyone's surprise,
Both men got up from the floor,
Looked at each other —
And slapped five!

Brother Jones

Brother Jones took to confessin'
One day at church,
Well, he confessed about his lying —
He confessed about his stealing —
But worse he confessed to all
the women he had in his life,
Brother Jones named so many women
He got the Reverend mad,
When Brother Jones was up to
his 20th —
The Reverend hollered out:
"Jones is you out there confessin'
Or you tryin' to brag?"

White Folks

White folks go to church
Can't even get 'em to smile,
Coloured folks go to church
You can hear 'em holler for miles!

Aunt Viola

Aunt Viola wore lovely dresses
And spoke in a cultured tongue,
And she owned a house in the suburbs,
And smiled politely at everyone.
But get Aunt Viola up home on
the weekend —
And let a little liquor free her tongue.
Next thing you know Aunt Viola's
On the kitchen table —
Shouting and doing the bump!

Mrs. Johnson

After Mrs. Johnson
Won the lottery,
With ticket number
880033,
Her house was suddenly besieged
By numerous people —
Claiming to be family.

The Association

One year in our community
The Association came to town,
People came from all over the province
From Amherst to Yarmouth —
From Sydney to Brindley Town,
Well, the preachin' and singing
was so good
People started shaking and generally losing their heads,
One lady from Digby had a heart attack
in the midst of a hallelujah —
And Rev. Septimus pronounced her dead.

Confession

When I was young
I used to hear a lot of ghosts,
And to tell you the truth
It was that more than being
a deacon's son —
That kept me a regular
in the Baptist Church.

Signs

She blamed it on stomach flu,
But nine months later —
Everybody knew.

Hallelujah Dave

Hallelujah Dave is pure misery
in church,
Cause he makes more noise
than any church service is worth.
When the Reverend takes the pulpit
And is just about to start
Hallelujah jumps from his seat and hollers:
"Lord, on your mark!"
And before the Reverend can say
a second word
Hallelujah shouts at the top of his lungs:
"Praise the Lord!"
And when the Reverend's almost finished
Just about to reach the end
Hallelujah's up with a big "Amen!"

DESIDERATA

DESIDERATUM

So much is in dispute here,
My trembling nerves are assaulted
by new threats,
My quest has opened a well of pain
Lying deep within the human flesh.

I run from this discovery
Opening to a huge landscape
But there is only the blank stare
Of a white moon
Washing me in its harsh rays,
And the crumbled image of Sphynx
Offering its faded fantasies
To the path of my eyes.

I refuse,
Standing on discovered knowledge —
Insisting on human resolve
Molding the self back into the human shape
that existed before I was carried off
Into the empire of cruel lies.

I am a standing figure —
Freed from the haunches of an old sleep
I arise —
Knowing that no more can come
From that old stance,
(The fear, self-hatred and fantasy
That kept me a slave)
No God exists in that stance —
And I must find God in the self —
And I insist that he be forever real.

LES NEGRES

The day enters the cavities
of evening,
And modern lights reveal
Wrecked souls and lost souls,
Who scream in their drunken frenzies
And hunger is the night.
But no longer in the folds of God,
or Love
or Family.
Their nerves are exposed
And they cannot
Drive one inspiration to point,
Assert one positive value,
Achieve any true meaning.
Hunger and need —
Deliver into the mouth,
Pain and hurt memories —
Deliver into the mouth,
Confusion and modernity —
Deliver into the mouth.
We must create to exist
It is our only solution,
Breathe new life into the dead caverns.
Create skilled crucibles out of substances of the dark.
Save we grow accustomed to bankrupt selves —
Shaped from relinquishments of old,
People who settle for less
And suffer in the cold.

THE GREEN HOUSE ON BIRMINGHAM STREET

The house is green,
It has 39 steps,
The steps crawl up to my
attic room,
As a spine crawls up
an old man's back,
The door opens like a tomb
Sounds ache from every step.

The house is old —
It leans heavily on a
wooden frame,
It holds together certain
faded memories,
There is dust and darkness
here
Eyes peep from every crack.

Mrs. Johnson lives in No. 7,
Mrs. Gray is in No. 4,
Harry McCormick rich and
bilious in No. 6,
Cecil Whynder — the black man
is in No. 5.

They have all admitted to lack
of success,
They have all relinquished
certain needed energies
And incline towards death.
I see them each evening
As they gather for ceremony:
playing cards, sipping tea,
I enter among them
Tossing perfunctory conversation
and smile,
And as my breath stirs the
dusty cavern
My thoughts whisper:
"Only I among them am
alive."

Summer droops to winter,
Leaves dissipate and fall,
And with each day's passage
The house leans more heavily
on its wooden frame,
The occupants discuss the quiver,
And after three years
I no longer seem to mind.

Mrs. Gray complains of her
indifferent brother,
Harry has a bad back,
Mrs. Johnson is silent and
mournful,
Cecil has not received his
cheque.
Tedious discussion to drown
the normal day,
Through which my image asserts
In its self-absorbed, anomalous way.
Climbing up the stairs —
Fixing my face to a smile,
Stop — chat — say goodbye,
Up again, until I arrive at
my own inglorious spot:
A 20 by 20 foot square
Burdened by erudite books
Bedazzled by modern art,
I peel off my clothes —
(As a lover peels off his clothes)
And delve into poetry:
(Eliot, Baraka, Yeats,)
Read aloud —
Perhaps too loudly,
Till a voice disturbs the
tender balance:
"There he goes again...reading poetry."
And what the voice says —
And how the voice says it —
Frightens me.

Rock this bastion of my youth,
Shake this sanctum at its
core,

The vague schemes to which
I so energetically adhere,
With a single crude voice
Now made hopelessly bare.

(And I had perceived myself
in the realm of great men,
And I had allowed this vision
to command,
Yet if one cares to examine
the empire:
A shabby palace attended
by the vulgar and moribund.)

I toss on clothes
And go into the streets,
Discarding long-held disguises
Seeking the common places of
relief:
Disco-dancing at "the Picadilly,"
Downing beer at "The Tap,"
Lingering among the prostitutes and
hustlers
that line the blocks of Hollis Street.
Yet coming down from it all
Amidst the tic toc of high-heels
Lonely voices trip and fall:
"I hate this stink place
I will not be back for a week."
"They tell me my friend has cancer,
And she is about to die."
"I feel a little low of late
Will you come to my place
for tea?"
"Oh my God," I soliloquize
"The world is made up of Harold McCormicks,
and Cecil Whynders and Mrs. Grays."

I return from these pursuits
in a mood made low,
Stamp the cold surface of streets —
Crawl through the door.
Up twenty steps — stop — chat,
Up nineteen more,

Pick up the phone
Pouring my heart through the
electric wires,
Explaining each aspect of
my pain
To someone who once listened to my
delicate desires,
But when her silence indicates
another failed quest,
I compose the mood and cuddle
a book against my chest.
And begin to read aloud
Perhaps deliberately,
Till a voice come up from
the underlying wood!
"There he goes again with the poetry —
I do believe the poor boy is lonely,
Cecil go up and invite him down
for tea."

The voices hush
and footsteps begin,
A chorus of screams and groans —
Pushed out of the wooden steps,
(Screams and groans that seem to be
pushed out of me,)
And the old man standing at my door —
Preparing for the ridiculous offer he will make
to someone like me,
I laugh when he begins:
His voice nervous and jingling as a key,
Though he has no need to worry —
I will greet him with a smile —
I will go to my fate willingly.

"Marika" (1988)

"Street Gathering" (1978)

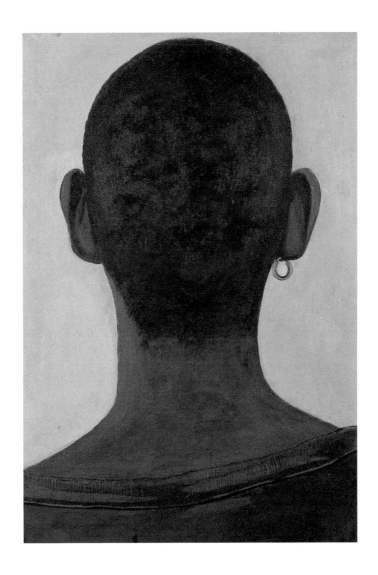

"Boy With Earring" (1988)

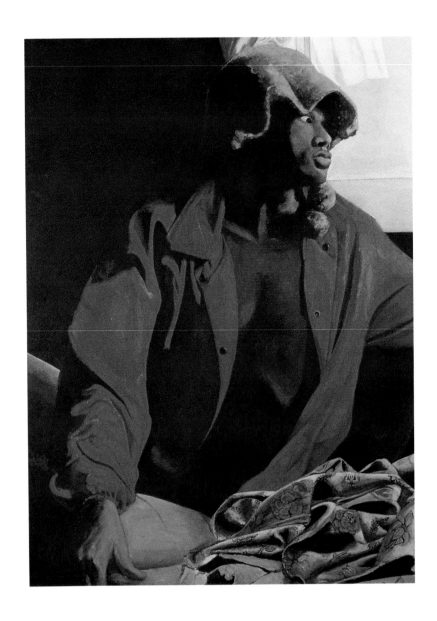

"Cain" (1988)

"Old Man" (1988)

"Les Gens" (1979)

"Aleeta" (1986)

"The Fiddler" (1988)

CONVERSATION WITH GILBERT

"You ask me why I am so willess?"
I sit in a tavern on Gottingen Street,
My head latched to a glass of beer,
Like a dog latched to the end of a leash,
And stare out from vacant eyes
Into scenes in which
I can no longer survive.
I turn to you in a solemn manner and say:
"Gilbert, I have this job in the South-end,
Going up each day
I take my place with the other fated actors,
Selling expensive electronic equipment:
TVs, stereos, VCRs, the like.
My fellow workers are quite
the kind —
Harry keeps the office laughing
with his comical anecdotes,
Ralph is into drugs and never
has much to say,
Jack's an intellectual
but really quite a bore,
Margaret, Jack's wife, just yesterday
grabbed me by the hand
And told me she was going insane."

The music pauses during my
delivery,
As if affected by something
opened by me,
And you begin
In a voice perfect for the ceremony:
"I carry on my charade
in the government building on
Hollis Street,
Designing social programs
for people on welfare, handicaps and
ethnic minorities,
I like my job a lot
And act rather astute,
But Mrs. James, my boss,
Is a fame-seeking, insecure

kind,
She's always meddling with my programs,
Sending in my reports late.
I hate her guts — but what the hell,
I've been there for 10 years —
I have a wife and kid now,
The job pays well."

Crude incidents press
into our outpourings,
Oblivious to all the finer desires
expressed by you and me,
At one table a dishevelled man
sits in a long, paralysed stare,
At another, a fight breaks out
over a spilled glass of beer,
At another an ugly woman argues
with her husband,
Who does not seem to care.

I raise my voice and continue:
"You and I have this problem.
It appears plain to me,
We cannot easily belong
or join this revelry,
Fired by notions of an
intense kind
We are maddened by each
passing moment
That does not free the ideals
From our burdened minds."

"I remember the old days," you respond,
"When you, me, Rocky and the boys
Marched for the causes
along these streets:
Gottingen, Falkland, Cunard,
We protested against racism,
We protested against poverty,
We protested against our murdered history.
We came here for celebration —
Surprised at how indifferent
the other faces remained.
Yet now irony of ironies —

Our faces have been added
to the sad characters
That line the tables of this
fateful scene."

His words leave me trembling,
Baring too much of a truth,
And I search
in my various stances —
For some new angle far us
to pursue,
But feeling a rush of blood, and feverish
tremors,
I dissolve into a world of fear,
And listen to an internal drama —
One which I can hardly bear:
A young, elegant man,
Gun in hand,
Turns and stares into my face
And demands:
"David, has the final word been spoken?
Have you truly resigned?
Is it really too late?"

I pick up and go into
the crowd,
Squeezing myself into puzzled faces,
Arranged sadly in chairs,
Slapping hands —
Exchanging superficial smiles,
Dancing in a most
ridiculous style,
Till a mirror catches me in its stare —
A long ridiculous figure transfixed
at the tail-end of a dream.

I return to my table —
Sit, order more beer.
"It is all about dedication isn't it?"
I turn to you and say,
"That unwavering devotion to purpose —
Despite all the incidents that distract,
All the challenges that continually
interrupt."

"And discipline," you add,
Or as we used to say in
the old days:
Let no hour of conscious
trial be wasted."
"I do not possess that stuff."
"And neither me," I respond.

The music overwhelms
the conversation,
Recognizing its final victory
I lift my glass
And offer a toast to you and
me.

"You ask my why I am
so willess?" I repeat,
Staring at my face flitting in the glass.
"I sit in a tavern on
Gottingen Street,
My head latched to a glass
of beer
Like a dog latched to the end of
a leash,
I like this tavern —
I like our conversations —
I like this last place of you
and me."

DECLARATION

Can I see the world
And myself in it?
A mind raped, battered,
tossed about by windy tricks.
There is nothing for me
in these grinning afternoons
With foolish men at the bar,
Or among the sad embraces of lonely women
in late-night rooms.
Or in the long walks through
the ruined avenues and futile stations
of the city.

I am alone —
and this is my fact,
A burning need drives me out
of dulled acquiescence,
To pound brains, belabour hands,
So as to master a huge intelligence
and lift out of a dying self.

I am often sitting in the blue afternoon,
Staring out of the window
That opens like a groggy eyelid
Onto the ruined expanse of human dreams,
With an aroused sense and animal impulse
To seize the throat of this bitter enterprise
And transform each atom of its frame
to perfection.

But with real eyes and real failings —
A harsh awareness ridicules the self
And presses the membranes back into
a quivering close.
(Life suspended by a thread
And a head that thinks too much
With no escape in love or fantasy.)

We must invent new words,
Master new situations,
Do new dances.
It is the necessity of

our salvation.
And we must assert new intelligence,
Construct a new order —
Explore new meaning —
And we must succeed!

EPITAPH
(for Kipoch Nojorge)

My friend Kipoch
Kenyan born,
Black as coal
From the Akamba tribe,
Has won an award —
and is off to New York,
After years of effort
He has begun to fly.

He is a riser in our
little town,
He is on the board of this
He is on the board of that,
He has appeared on local
television,
He is known by politicians.

Kipoch has a vision
And it disturbs him day by day,
He must succeed!
He must succeed!
He is strict in his manner
He works slavishly,
He has improved his English
He has earned two degrees.

He is from Ikutha village
In Kenya's east,
His people are diseased and
strife-torn,
But he will not talk of that
now
He no longer writes to his
family,
He can no longer bear discussion
of his country.

Kipoch makes speeches
Whenever given a chance,
Among whites — he is known
to produce tears,

He does his native dances
For their amusement,
At night he is restless
and possessed by fear.

When black people in
the North-end began to
uprise,
Kipoch was quick to reproach:
"The world is ruled by a new
order of men:
The educated, the diligent,
One should not be fooled
by these lazy people
Or cloud the mind with
racial sympathies."

When a group of refugees
washed up along the shore,
Kipoch was even more
severe:
"These men are the flotsam
of troubled spots,
To allow them in the country
is to inherit their lowly woes,
And corrupt all we have achieved here."

I see him in a halo
of gold,
Standing in a brightened
ceremony,
Receiving applause from those
Who consider him extraordinary.

He will be standing there.
("Tucked" in tuxedo
Fixed in smile)
Standing there trembling and alone.

Once slavery took 15 million
men and women,
Raped and tortured their souls,
Kipoch is a modern type
He goes and serves willingly.

FOR OLD MEN ON GOTTINGEN STREET

In September's morning
I have considered the cold
press of feet,
Through the banal avenues of city,
And the sad faces of old men
on concrete steps —
Singing out of old guitars,
While the modern world
Lifts its limbs of terror,
And frightens these tiny caverns
Where the weak remain alive.

I have looked into such places —
And heard old voices shout,
But the noises rise from
other places,
And they are drowned and
unheard again.

It is their flesh I feel with me —
Rubbing against each aspect
of myself,
Bullying me with each uncovering
of knowledge
To save old men
In their drunken wills.

Their hands quiver —
Their eyes are mouths that shout,
"Ahh! you think that you understand,
But with a simple twist of fate
We are you my son.
We could have known sun!"

And their lives repeat
at each turn along my way,
Till I can find no peace
And I discover the horror inside
the ordinary day.

And it is not that they are black —
But that they are black and broken,

And it is not that they are dying —
But that they were the hopes of the dead,
And it is not that they are frightening —
But that their fate molests me
like a knife.

EXECUTION

The passions of youth
Exhaust in lust-filled
corners,
Unable, after the heat
to recover,
God, Sun, Moon disappoint,

We do not prepare our children
for their quest,
We set them up
Set them up — for death,
Line their bodies
against waiting walls,
Without shields — real bullets
hit them
And they fall.

APEX/NADIR

We possess hours and music
and curtains of memories,
But that does not make us
legitimate.

When you see those
Who have left the discipline
Of family or institution,
You realize the lie.

The world consists of the compromise
After the principle is deserted,
The world consists of the lie
In the midst of seductive
masks.

After one room is conquered —
There is the upkeep,
Unless systems ease such a
path
There will be repetition of the wrong.
After the organized thrust into existence,
Comes the long-practised chaos.

OUT-TOWN

Can we stand against time?
In this cage held in old misery,
Warmed by a decaying God —
Who has never delivered us out
of backwardness and poverty.

We laugh in old ritual
Umbilical attachments of the soul,
Uncle Tony's energetic dances
Grandma's ebullient laughter,
Banjo music and comedic
ravings,
Attachments that maintain a romantic notion
That a place can exist wholly apart
Requiring only the single talent
of human love.

But drunken men, and flamboyant cars
and brutalized women,
Vomit like a sick dog on this paradise,
And young children — babies in their
stomachs
Show how defenceless we are,
How wild and ridiculous
we can become,
When we desert truth —
And cease to be responsible for
the modern world.

Refuse the romance of the brain,
Look beyond the heavenly gaze —
Read history and see,
From the time of the Loyalists
to now
What this has always been:
A battered people tossed into obscene pits,
Made poor, dulled of drive, stupefied.
Dragged into the modern world on
a hook of cruelty,
Losing eyes. No longer able to see.

Voices thick with the accent of oppression
Are more honest and reveal,
Songs alive with the pain of slavery
Are more honest and reveal,
Old houses — emaciated and decayed
are more honest and reveal,
The sadness that still breathes
in this land,
Of a people lost to themselves,
Unable to command,
Moving flamboyantly through the edifices of
modern cities,
People who long ago could not stand
the pain,
And escaped into a fantasy image
of self
That now leaves them odd, and stunted,
And emersed in complete misery.

THE HOWL
(For Newfoundland)

To issue inside bare rooms
A howl — leaping hot and red
into the midnight air,
And issued it again —
Banging against the door
of impossible dreams,
With a baggage of pain
and lost feeling,
Flooding the veins of blackened flesh.

Man, man must end this state,
of men of colour — raped,
Taken out of selves,
Lashed together like logs,
Dragged to the ends of the earth
To lap at civilized dreams,
Tied hopelessly to a post
Whipped — whipped mercilessly,
Until there is nothing left to attach
the meat to
Nothing real.

St. John's, Newfoundland,
White city in earth heaven,
Concrete and asphalt and
tentacled streets,
Fishing villages and rowed houses
Tossing exhausted smoke into
the morning air,
And old men with eyes like hooks
Limping their way to corner stores,
A wealth of faces and a wealth
of gestures,
And occasional incident that offends,
But the face of island —
Bare, lazy, indifferent.

These people do not love me,
These edifices are not the energetic
constructions of my hands,
Nor their talk — the vibrant

language of my mind.
I can only be caught — like
frenzied fish,
In the wide net of their definitions,
I can only beat — like fish
at the end of hooks,
Till my energies exhaust
And I am served up with the
morning meal,
To mouths that eat me alive.

I could die in a place like this,
Die in one of these rowed houses
On LeMarchant Street,
As the morning rises above the
blackened roofs,
And the neighbours begin their daily chatter and coffee.

Die — Finding myself sprawled
out on a bed,
Inspected by rows of eyes
Who look in but cannot explain —
Except for an old dotard
Relating her exaggerated tales,
Excited by the drama that
has brought her to life.

Die — unable to inspire monument
or memory,
Sympathy or grief,
Among minds that quickly rise and
recede
Like the waves that surge in useless forays
out of the belly of the sea.

The creature rebels —
And will not continue
Along the vast shores of emptiness,
Spread like a cloth
Over the ball of my eyes,
Rebels — and releases a howl.
A howl that lifts out of the dying houses
and chattering hallways,
Races over shadowed parks, and dusty streets,

Climbs up among the tarred roofs
and smoking chimneys,
Fierce in its mission,
To awake a sleeping world.
But fails — fails at last,
Hardly heard
Among the rocks waves and
content dramas
of Newfoundland.

CHORUS FROM STONE

If after numerous visits
There is no point,
Then why go?
The music twisting in a sensual corner,
Indulges the moment
Yet cannot overcome the fear.

And if bowing to a great passion
One sees a path of ruination,
Why insist?

Is it not obvious —
One cannot achieve usefulness
in a nothing?
Reap harvest from a desert?
Though the passions are served
Quickly in a room,
The self wastes regardless.

Lift the eyes from bondage
Shift the angle and see:
To lay still is to die,
To go without direction
is to lie,
To learn without conviction
is to assume,
To seek without an ultimate
Is to merely protrude.

Steal energy from the air
Hush an ego
Devote a corpuscle
To a cause completely worthy,
To a principle incredibly sacred,
To a need completely justified,
Cast off idle indulgences —
Give meaning to life!

MACHUKIO (The Terror)

What is not given in love
Is not worth it.
What feeds the bones of sad men
Is not the ability to procure,
Prostitutes are not sought as wives —
Mothers are the most loved.

Each fragment lying outside
The structure of love
Turns to monster in the late night,
Each society that discards people
Sharpens hands for killing.

And as we lay in the abandoned expanse —
Pressed into negative instincts,
Pray for God to seize us completely,
Lest we give in to the sentence
Of those lost to hope, giving in to despair,
Who hunger for their own deaths —
To which they go without tears.

ARTIFACT

(For Rose)

It is never good to agree
to hands choking you to death.

A runner stretches limbs
across huge plains,
A thinker calls to ancient works,
A student is inculcated on
astute books.

It is never good to agree
to your own triviality —
Pressing you into a status
of nothing,
And being warm in that
status,
As if wrapped by a great, sacred prize.

Our institutions take breath
and move on,
Grow to power on wills that
forge on,
While you stay in a dumb
of will
That keeps the eyes closed —
And refuses the sensational intelligence
of the new world.

RHYME FOR A DIME

At the Ebony Club
It is easy to see,
How the game is played,
How lives dizzy with
passion,
Arrange in pattern
on the floor.

The music that seizes
the air,
The wine that wraps
the head,
keeps us to the system
While we dance
Our enemies are diligent
and move without fear.

And on the floor
Those with power
Stand and collect at the door,
Those with some
pass quick judgments on those
on the dance floor,
And those with none
Party on down!

THE HYPOCRITES AND THE POET

"The people are poor,"
Said the businessman,
"And so we need money
to save them."

"The people are stupid and illiterate,"
said the educator,
"And so we need more money to improve their minds."

"The people are oppressed
and without voice," said the
politician,
"And so we need more money
To elevate them from their plight."

"But the people are warm and beautiful,
And hug me tight in family,"
Said the poet,
"They need only love!"

The businessman received money
And with quick hands constructed
a huge, ridiculous building
with expensive machines
and smiling secretaries —
That produced absolutely nothing,
And a later scandal revealed
He had helped himself generously
To an immense salary, new car
and vacations for his family.

The educator received money
And conducted elaborate research
on the "Whyfores" of this
and the "Wherefores" of that,
That proved little more than
what was already known,
And he was showered with praise,
And his edition bound in gold,
Only then to be committed to shelves
to collect dust,

While the people remained puzzled and astray
In institutions that ruined them.

The politician received money,
And quickly gobbled it up
on gambling debts,
Though careful manner and
timely speeches,
Enabled him to maintain his stature
among the poor,
Though a few more aware
Challenged his name in public,
And caused him in private moments
to say:
"Look at these goddamned people,
They're not worth a goddamned thing."

The poet received none —
But the fierce honesty
of his words,
Opened doors inside the
people's minds,
And they flocked to see him
and listened intently to his words,
And with new inspiration —
They constructed buildings, wrote new books.
And the people and the poet
Learned from each other and grew immensely,
And they did it with love,
And only love.

REUBEN JONES, B.A.

This is the story of Reuben Jones,
Son of Deacon Wilfred Jones and
Whilemina Jones,
Flaunted by reverend and senior
deacon alike —
To be the most gifted in our community —
The most exemplary of our kind.

He attended university
Obtained a B.A.
Got a job at the local bank
And quickly descended into the following
type:
He wore spectacular suits
and fronted a chauvinistic smile,
He would not endear himself to a woman
Unless she was white,
He would not "hang" with "the boys"
They were simply not his type,
He would not live in the community
It was too backward and poor,
He would not attend our church —
He had no use for religion
as before.

At age 35 he was caught in an attempt
to embezzle a company,
He spent two years in jail and
came out quite miserably,
His wife — equally shallow
Immediately left,
His house was taken by the mortgage
company,
His car sold to pay off debts.

To complete the story:
He returned to his mother's house
up home,
Drove truck for a
garbage company,
And appeared incessantly harassed
and alone.

Strange, it seems
For one elevated to such heights
A few years before,
That his story now feeds conversations
From the church to the corner store,
A comment quickly arrived at
By both wise and foolish
Those near and far,
Of the sad fate of those
Who in reaching for the world
Discard the most important thing:
Who they are.

Native Song

ANTHEM

For a man to know himself
Feel the rages of history,
Discover a mammoth idea
and move to its fulfilling moment.

To uncover a passion for the hands,
Find a contest worthy of honest
energy,
Be attached to the love of
humanity,
Marry a conviction
Live — and love life continually.

THE ONUS

When there is no choice
And need excavates to deeper
emotions,
And the tide swells to new
consternation,
And conviction seizes the throat,
And simplicity is abandoned for
complex devotion,
And ease for more difficult task,
And breathing is blood and guts for life,
Then we will know it, we will know it.

VISION

The world should push itself toward the sun,
There is heaven in most men's eyes,
It is not green or metallic
Nor concerned with black and white.

The world should remember
That love does not depend on possession
Of a beautiful image
Or submission to another man's eyes,
But merely begins with the heart's consent.

The world should think of its children,
Who hopped and skipped in the garden,
Till a thick mist of hate came to
choke their eyes.

APPEARANCES
(For Mr. Dolan)

Until they come to disturb
our world,
See what joys we can scrape
From these clandestine meetings
of the soul,
And energetic discussion of triangle,
square and rectangle shapes,
With honest laughter to fill the air,
And the occasional "faux-pas"
as we down the beer,
Till a knock is heard
And we quickly fall in line,
And I again become the radical
And you, Mr. Dolan, adjust your tie.

BEECHVILLE
(For Ronnie Wright)

Images of young passage
Black, huddled below walls,
Struggling for confidence
in the wind and white storms,
Blowing about a Nova Scotia coast.

The streets sense wisdom
and call out:
"These ways were born to pain
These ways were hardened in the
rock of despair and shame,
Bring new life to these veins — my boy,
I offer you a challenge."

Leaned back into conversation
With old men and women,
Drunk, strumming on guitars,
Voices sweet with ideals never
touched in real life
But hugged tightly in the soul,
Old desires wanting new flames —
Old dreams wanting new energies.
And a boy-self becoming man
Stuck like a cloth into its soul,
Turned in its emotions
Till imbibed
He walks through the avenues of city
Alive with new instruction.

INSTRUCTION
(For Nova Scotia)

The trouble that inhabits the day,
Throws up tragic images that
quickly betray,
The elegant posturing of your ways.

Toss an eye back — you will understand,
Each nerve must be loved or sprout
ugly seeds,
Or grow gaunt and elongated,
Or incline too much like old women.

Love like the sun —
So it is clear.

Nova Scotia,
Love your children — all of them.
Give them a place in your
gilded palaces,
As quickly as you offer space
in your public spots,
Open them with your waters
Or they will die.
For what face forms after rejection?
What beast emerges after the rape
of pride?

Judges will come to assess your kingdom —
Will toss an eye behind your cultured words,
and energetic braggings,
Will apportion honour and praise
Will reveal your ruthlessness and disgrace.
Will stick a ray into your hidden
places
And reveal — how elegant dress
Often decorates a ruthless man,
How a sophisticated language
often conceals a heinous crime.

SUMMONS
(For Africville)

Truth stands a sceptre of stone
Amidst all the clever deceptions
our modern society posits,
Our lives with anger burn
Pricked by the smell and negation
of garbage pits.

Crass rulers of our society
announce
All the casual observations the
powerful announce,
And our hopes are drowned again
In the welter of the modern
word.

Listen —
Let us disrupt the lie,
When we see our child-beauty
parade her naked flesh,
Or when we see our kingdom of love
Brought to an ignoble death,
And when we feel the slow acid
invade our veins,
And realize —
We had love — Love above all
To conquer this bitter terrain.

Let us gain mad-wisdom,
Let us not allow our beauty
to sink to low pits,
Or our sun to be dulled
by sullied blankets,
Let us rebel against this lie
Lift up an intelligent sword
and assault the new world.

FOSSILIZATION

Maybe this earth is a failed task —
Why hide behind a mask?
Faces steeped in sorrow show
While powerful walk the earth
Dragging the entrails of frightened men:
The poor in horrible oppression,
The intelligent in vaulted prisons —
unable to come out.

That we find fault with God
Is not the true concern,
Has darkness ever willed us
to oblivion?
Or winter exhausted the determined flame?

Or that we persist in
miraculous expectation —
Is not our greatest loss.

Do you think the old principle
has been deserted,
Of men bent on final instincts —
Ignited to virtuous task,
One erects Elysium in the
walls of Hell,
Another paints scenes of blinding beauty
on a stone roof,
Another rises to gargantuan efforts
for the elevation of his people.

We must re-kindle dead fires,
Set new standards for the coming age.
It may not be that we no longer
have a God
But that we require new sacrifice
To give him status over this
disturbed age.

NATIVE SONG
(For Cyril & Rosella Fraser)

We find ourselves in purpose steeped,
To wrestle pain from these tired hands,
And erect new hope in the dark
horizon,
Beyond the reach of those who command.

A racist man's tools —
His education, his erudite words,
Have kept us closed,
We are not relieved by ecstatic
devotion to God,
Or by easy wish,
Despite all involvements
An agonized cry still emits from the soul.

Old men and old women
Know of the horror of those days,
When young and dressed in Sunday-fine,
They made their way to town,
And were fixed contemptuously
by white eyes —
Hounded from dust till dawn
Till their hopes were crushed,
And their sense of freedom died.

And drunk remembrances of old men
Of old days and old glories,
Or Mom Suse, Pearleen Oliver
that type,
Whose love rose like a sun
through the miasmal haze.

Yet as we wander in bowed status,
In minds estranged from themselves,
Dance as we always dance
In the old hall, or late-night club
What song shall rise from the
throat?
What great task will seize the hands?

And if that Preston man in inspired
vision
had not set about to construct
his itinerant church,
Or Mrs. Best — awakened by study —
Had not asserted her womanly pride,
Or that Jones man had not considered and
meant his violence,
What would we be then?
Cadavers arranged like logs
Moving along a stink river
Not ours
But flowing on — lost forever.

An acrid mist rises above the land,
The sad breath of mother earth,
Tired of having weaned children
in deep cradles of human love:
Lucasville, Sunnyville, North Preston,
Weymouth Falls,
Children who are abandoned
And are left sad without choice.

I will go on my way
With a clear conviction,
To break these Nova Scotian
chains
So that a girl can decide
in a real way
To seize the earth by storm,
Or to sit back quietly into
the bosom of earth,
Nurtured by a long and ancient
love.
And I will fight — as wickedly
as the devil fights,
All that stifles her breath.

And when the sun settles
like a tired eyelid —
On the failed promise of Preston,
And ghosts of old appear,
I will sing a song
And that song will be beautiful,

And that song will be great,
And no man on earth will be able
to block it from his ears.
And this will be my monument
Collected from the beauty and
pain,
Of all those who have lived
and died
In the hungry chambers
of the black dream.

NOTES

(Arranged according to appearance in the text.)

Preston - The largest of Nova Scotia's over 30 black communities. It was settled by Loyalist Blacks in 1783 onwards and by Refugee Blacks after 1812. Preston is made up of three black settlements: North Preston, East Preston and Cherrybrook. The community lies about 25 miles east of Halifax.

Rev. Richard Preston - Black religious leader in the mid-1800s. He founded over 12 "Black Churches" in Nova Scotia and in 1854, organized them into the African Baptist Association.

The After-Hours, The Derby, The Ebony Connection, the Picadilly, The Tap - Nightclubs, taverns frequented by blacks in Halifax.

Hammonds Plains - Small semi-rural black community just outside Halifax

The Square - Uniacke Square, a city housing project in the north-end of Halifax.

Guysborough County - One of Nova Scotia's least developed counties. It contains several small black communities.

Bridgetown, Middleton - Small towns in the Annapolis Valley region of Nova Scotia.

North Preston - The largest of the "Preston" Black communities.

Weymouth Falls - Rural black community in southern Nova Scotia.

Creighton Ave. - Site of a small black settlement, in Dartmouth, N.S.

Gottingen St. - The central street in the north end of Halifax.

"Rocky," "Jones-man" - "Rocky" Jones, a noted black political activist and historian.

Falkland, Cunard Streets - Streets in north-end of Halifax

Beechville - Semi-rural black community outside Halifax

Mrs. Best - Dr. Carrie Best a noted civil rights activist, newspaper editor, and author from New Glasgow N.S.

Mom Suse - Prior to her death 1987, the oldest living black resident of Nova Scotia.

Pearleen Oliver - Religious leader among black women

The Association - Annual gathering of Black Baptist Churches in Nova Scotia.

PLAYS BY DAVID WOODS

For Elsie Dorrington
Voices
The Dream Continues
The Meeting
Dream of a Child
A Song for Papa George
Amy's Big Decision
Allison In Blackland
The March

BIOGRAPHICAL SKETCH

David Woods was born on the island of Trinidad in the West Indies. He emigrated to Canada in 1972 at age 12, and settled with his family in Dartmouth Nova Scotia. He attended Dartmouth High School and later Dalhousie University, where he studied Political Science. In 1977 he was one of the organizers of the now defunct Black Youth Organization, a group dedicated to the uplifting of the black community and articulating the needs of black youth. This began his long and varied involvement in the black community of Nova Scotia. David has served as program director of the Black United Front and the Black Cultural Centre. In 1983 he founded the Cultural Awareness Youth Group of Nova Scotia — a provincial youth organization dedicated to the cultural, education, and social development of black youth in Nova Scotia. Under his leadership the organization was awarded the prestigious Commonwealth Youth Service Award in 1986, recognizing it as one of the most innovative youth-service agencies in the Commonwealth.

David has also been active in the arts. He has written and staged his own plays including *Voices* (chosen to represent Canada at an international youth festival in 1986) *The Dream Continues*, and *For Elsie Dorrington*. He has acted on local stages in dramas such as Athol Fugard's *Master Harold and The Boys*. He has appeared in film (most recently *Journey Into Darkness: The Bruce Curtis Story*). He has written for radio and television. As well, David is an accomplished artist. In 1980 he represented Nova Scotia as an artist in Canada's first-ever National Black Arts Conference. His paintings were recently seen in the CBC film, "In Service," based on a story by Maxine Tynes.

David currently resides in Halifax where he splits his time between painting, writing and working as a program consultant for the Halifax City Regional Library. This is David's first collection of poetry.